Community Places

Post Office

by Amy McDonald

Blastoff! Beginners

BELLWETHER MEDIA
MINNEAPOLIS, MN

Blastoff! Beginners are developed by literacy experts and educators to meet the needs of early readers. These engaging informational texts support young children as they begin reading about their world. Through simple language and high frequency words paired with crisp, colorful photos, Blastoff! Beginners launch young readers into the universe of independent reading.

Sight Words in This Book

are	is	this	you
at	people	to	
get	the	too	
have	these	up	
in	they	we	

This edition first published in 2022 by Bellwether Media, Inc.

Library of Congress Cataloging-in-Publication Data

Names: McDonald, Amy, 1985- author.
Title: Post office / by Amy McDonald.
Description: Minneapolis, MN : Bellwether Media, 2022. | Series: Blastoff! beginners : community places | Includes bibliographical references and index. | Audience: Ages PreK-2 | Audience: Grades K-1
Identifiers: LCCN 2021044270 (print) | LCCN 2021044271 (ebook) | ISBN 9781644875698 (library binding) | ISBN 9781648346606 (paperback) | ISBN 9781648345807 (ebook)
Subjects: LCSH: Postal service--Juvenile literature. | Post office stations and branches--Juvenile literature.
Classification: LCC HE6078 .M398 2022 (print) | LCC HE6078 (ebook) | DDC 383--dc23
LC record available at https://lccn.loc.gov/2021044270
LC ebook record available at https://lccn.loc.gov/2021044271

Editor: Christina Leaf Designer: Andrea Schneider

Printed in the United States of America, North Mankato, MN.

Table of Contents

At the Post Office!

We have letters
to send.
We are at
the post office!

United States
Post Office
T THE POST OFFICE
NG LABELS,
E AND MORE.
8501

What Are Post Offices?

Post offices are busy places. They move mail.

mail

People send mail
at the post office.
They get mail, too!

Services
Insurance
Delivery Confirmation
Signature Confirmation
Registered Mail
Certified Mail
Return Receipt

Moving Mail

This is the **lobby**.
People wait
in line.

PACKAGING
CHOOSE THE FLAT RATE BOX OR ENVELOPE RIGHT FOR YOU
LARGE
MEDIUM
MEDIUM
SMALL
Passport
here.
Photos & Expedited Service also available.
PASSPORTS

lobby

This is the **counter**. People send **packages**.

counter

These are mailboxes. People drop in letters to send.

United States
Post Office
FARRAGUT POST OFFICE
1800 M ST
WASHINGTON DC 20036
Welcome
mailboxes
UNITED STATES POSTAL SERVICE

These are **PO Boxes**. People pick up mail.

PO Boxes

This is the sorting room. Workers get mail ready.

sorting room

These are mail trucks. They bring mail to YOU!

www.usps.com
www.usps.com

Post Office Facts

Inside a Post Office

What Happens at a Post Office?

send packages

get mail from PO Boxes

send letters

Glossary

counter

the place in a post office where workers help people

lobby

a room for customers at the post office

packages

items sent in boxes

PO Boxes

places to pick up mail at the post office

To Learn More

ON THE WEB

FACTSURFER

Factsurfer.com gives you a safe, fun way to find more information.

1. Go to www.factsurfer.com.
2. Enter "post office" into the search box and click 🔍.
3. Select your book cover to see a list of related content.

Index

The images in this book are reproduced through the courtesy of: Rick Lewis/ Alamy, front cover; Ljupco Smokovski, p. 3; Trong Nguyen, pp. 4-5; Quang Ho, p. 6; Alex Segre/ Alamy, pp. 6-7; David R. Frazier Photolibrary/ Alamy, pp. 8-9; Joni Hanebutt, pp. 10-11; Fototocam, p. 12; Jeffrey Isaac Greenberg 3+/ Alamy, pp. 12-13; Hiram Rios, pp. 14-15; Jim Craigmyle/ Getty Images, pp. 16-17; Reuters/ Alamy, pp. 18-19; Greg K_ca, p. 20; Jillian Cain, pp. 20-21; Jeffrey Isaac Greenberg 13+/ Alamy, p. 22 (inside); Rocketclips, Inc., p. 22 (send packages); l i g h t p o e t, p. 22 (get mail); Cebolla4, p. 22 (send letters); Jeff Greenberg/ age fotostock/ SuperStock, p. 23 (counter); Tupungato, p. 23 (lobby); New Africa, p. 23 (packages); hanohiki, p. 23 (PO Boxes).